1. Introduction:

In their famous 1984 paper, Shapiro & Stiglitz (hereafter S&S) developed what has become the canonical efficiency wage model.[1] The premise of the model is that high effort can be induced if workers are paid "efficiency" wages high enough that they fear losing their jobs and so choose not to shirk. The main result of the paper is that unemployment always exists in equilibrium; if there were no unemployment, then a fired worker could find another job right away at the same wage, and so there could be no wage high enough to induce non-shirking.

In their paper, S&S assume that workers who put forth low effort are completely unproductive, so the only way for a firm to hire effective labor is to pay an efficiency wage and induce non-shirking. In contrast, I treat the effective labor provided by a shirking worker as a parameter γ that is allowed to vary from zero (shirkers provide no effective labor) to one (shirkers provide as much effective labor as a non-shirkers).[2] If shirkers are productive, then there are two ways to hire a unit of effective labor: offer a single "good" job, meaning a job that pays an efficiency wage and where shirking is punished by firing; or to offer $1/\gamma$ "bad" jobs, meaning jobs where workers are allowed/expected to shirk.

The first goal of this paper is to show that it is possible for only good jobs to be offered in equilibrium (as in S&S); but it is also possible for only bad jobs, or for some good jobs and some bad jobs, to be offered in equilibrium. Specifically, I show that if γ is sufficiently small, then firms will always find it cheaper to hire a unit of effective labor by offering one good job and paying an efficiency wage than by offering $1/\gamma$ bad jobs, so only good jobs will be offered in

---

[1] A small sample of the theoretical research inspired by this paper includes Bulow & Summers (1986), Levine (1989), MacLeod & Malcomson (1998), and Strand (1987).
[2] In both the S&S model and the present one, workers are all identical; they do not vary in their disutility of effort. So whether or not workers shirk depends entirely on the incentives they face.

equilibrium.[3] Similarly, if γ is sufficiently large, firms will always find it cheaper to offer $1/\gamma$ bad jobs than to offer one good job, so only bad jobs will be offered in equilibrium (i.e., *all* workers in the economy will shirk). For intermediate values of γ, firms will be indifferent between offering one good job and offering $1/\gamma$ bad jobs, and there will be a positive number of both good jobs and bad jobs in equilibrium.

It is worth noting that the threshold level of γ below which only good jobs are offered, and the threshold level of γ above which only bad jobs are offered, are functions of labor demand. I show that as labor demand becomes arbitrarily high the threshold level of γ below which only good jobs are offered approaches zero; the higher is labor demand, the more unproductive shirkers must be for no employers to want to offer any bad jobs.[4] The intuition is that when labor demand is very high, the efficiency wage becomes very high as well, while the cost of offering $1/\gamma$ bad jobs and filling them with unemployed workers stays constant, as these workers only need to be paid enough to compensate them for their foregone leisure.

Similarly, I show that as labor demand becomes arbitrarily high the threshold of γ above which only bad jobs are offered approaches one; the higher is labor demand the more productive shirkers must be for no employers to want to offer any good jobs.[5] The intuition for this relies on the fact that the magnitude of the efficiency wage depends on how much utility a fired worker gets. In the S&S equilibrium, a fired worker gets the utility that comes from being unemployed. But if bad jobs exist, then a worker fired from a good job can get the utility associated with having a bad job. If there is unemployment in the economy, then the bad-job wage is just enough to make workers indifferent between having a bad job (and shirking) and being unemployed, and so

---

[3] This is consistent with the S&S paper. While formally they assume that shirkers produce no output, they point out that their equilibrium will hold if shirkers have productivity that is positive but sufficiently low.
[4] No bad jobs will ever be offered if $\gamma = 0$, regardless of the level of labor demand.
[5] No good jobs will ever be offered if $\gamma = 1$, regardless of the level of labor demand; if shirkers are just as productive as non-shirkers, there is no benefit to paying an efficiency wage to induce non-shirking.

the bad-job wage is just equal to the cost of foregone leisure. But if there is full employment in the economy--if everyone who does not have a good job has a bad job--then the bad-job wage will be higher than this. It turns out that a one dollar increase in the bad-job wage causes a one dollar increase in the efficiency wage, so a one-dollar increase in the bad-job wage makes hiring a unit of effective labor by offering one good job increase by a dollar, but makes hiring a unit of effective labor by offering $1/\gamma$ bad jobs more expensive by $1/\gamma > 1$ dollars, making it more attractive to offer a good job.

For intermediate values of γ, neither the condition for only good jobs to be offered nor the condition for only bad jobs to be offered holds; if all firms were offering only good jobs, a firm would prefer to replace one good job with $1/\gamma$ bad jobs, and if all firms were offering only bad jobs, a firm would prefer to replace $1/\gamma$ bad jobs with one good job. In these cases, there exists an intermediate equilibrium in which there are a positive number of both good jobs and bad jobs, and firms are indifferent between offering one good job and $1/\gamma$ bad jobs.

The second goal of this paper is to show the results of two sets of comparative statics exercises. The first set involves the effect of changes in labor demand on employment and wages (in both good and bad jobs), as well as on total effective labor supplied. As in the original S&S paper, increasing labor demand when only good jobs are offered in equilibrium causes the number of good jobs, the good-job wage, and total effective labor supplied to increase. Increasing labor demand when only bad jobs are offered in equilibrium either causes an increase in employment and output, but no change in wages (if demand is sufficiently low that there is unemployment in the economy), or it causes an increase in bad-job wages, but no change in employment or output (if demand is high enough that there is full employment in the economy).

Increasing labor demand when both good and bad jobs are offered in equilibrium and there is unemployment causes the number of bad jobs and output to increase. The additional workers are drawn from the unemployment pool, so the bad-job wage, and hence the good-job wage, remain constant, but the average wage falls. If there is full employment in the economy, then an increase in labor demand causes the number of good jobs to rise, the number of bad jobs to fall, and both kinds of wages (and average wages) and total effective labor supplied to rise. The intuition is that when labor demand is higher, there is no way to expand total employment (because everyone has a job), but higher demand makes it worthwhile to increase good-job wages by enough to convert some bad-job workers into good-job workers.

This comparative statics analysis may have some relevance for the empirical literature on cyclicality of wages. That literature has found mixed results regarding whether wages are pro-cyclical.[6] The present model contains testable predictions about when wages should be pro-cyclical, counter-cyclical, or a-cyclical, and may help to resolve the ambiguity in the empirical literature.

The second set of comparative statics exercises involves the effect of changes in γ. Increasing γ has no effect at all if only good jobs are offered in equilibrium. If only bad jobs are offered in equilibrium and there is unemployment in the economy, then an increase in γ will cause the total amount of effective labor supplied to increase (shirking workers will be more productive), and the effect on employment will be ambiguous (total effective labor supplied is higher, but each shirking worker is more productive). If only bad jobs are offered in equilibrium and there is full employment, than an increase in γ can have no effect on employment, will cause total effective labor supplied to increase, and has an ambiguous effect on the bad-job wage.

---

[6] See Abraham and Haltiwanger (1995) for a survey.

If there are a positive number of both good jobs and bad jobs, the equilibrium condition requires that firms be indifferent between offering one good job and offering $1/\gamma$ bad jobs. If there is unemployment in equilibrium, then the bad-job wage is fixed at the level just sufficient to induce unemployed workers to accept jobs and shirk. The good-job wage is fixed at $1/\gamma$ times this level, which means that the number of good jobs is fixed as well. Total effective labor increases; the number of good jobs does not change and workers in bad jobs become more productive. The effect on the number of bad jobs is ambiguous; output from bad jobs increases, but each bad-job worker has become more productive. If there are a positive number of good jobs and bad jobs and there is no unemployment in equilibrium, then offering bad jobs becomes more attractive relative to offering good jobs, so the number of bad jobs increases and the number of good jobs falls. The effects on total effective labor, bad-job wages, and good-job wages are ambiguous.

This comparative statics exercise points out an unexplored possible consequence of technological change. If the change takes the form of making shirkers more productive, then its effect on wages, output, and employment will depend on which equilibrium the economy is in. More generally, the effect of a technological improvement will depend on the effect is has on the productivity of shirkers relative to that of non-shirkers.

The remainder of the paper is organized as follows. Section 2 develops a baseline model that is almost identical to the original Shapiro & Stiglitz (S&S) model. Section 3 introduces into the model the possibility of shirkers with productive output, and describes how the number of good jobs and the number of bad jobs offered in equilibrium depends on γ. Section 3 also contains the comparative statics exercises. Section 4 describes the empirical implications of the model. Section 5 concludes.

2. The Shapiro & Stiglitz (S&S) Model:

The model described in this section is essentially a restatement of S&S, except that I use a discrete-time framework instead of continuous time. Except where stated otherwise, all of the results in this section are the same as in S&S.

A. Setup.

N identical infinitely-lived workers each have a per period utility function $U = w - e$ where w is the wage received and e is the level of effort exerted on the job. Workers maximize the expected present value of their lifetime utility stream, where utility in future periods is discounted at rate r. S&S assume that shirkers contribute nothing to output. Employed workers can exert high effort e_H, or can shirk and exert some minimal level of effort e_L. S&S normalize e_L to zero. I allow it to be positive but strictly lower than e_H.

An unemployed worker receives unemployment utility $\bar{u}$ and puts forth no effort. There is some probability b that an employed worker will have an exogenous job separation (and be forced into the unemployment pool) in a particular period.

The only decision made by an individual employed worker is whether or not to shirk. High effort is always efficient (i.e., $1 - e_H > \gamma - e_L$). All workers caught shirking are fired.[7] A shirker has some exogenous probability q of being caught in a particular period. An unemployed worker has a probability a of being hired into a new job in a particular period. This probability is endogenous as it depends on the (also endogenous) unemployment rate.

---

[7] This is an optimal strategy for firms. In equilibrium, an individual firm can hire as many non-shirking workers as it wishes at the going wage. Firms are therefore indifferent between tolerating a shirker and firing the shirker and hiring another worker out of the unemployment pool. If a firm perceives even an infinitesimal value of punishing shirking (such as acquiring a reputation for toughness), then it will strictly prefer to do so.

A worker who habitually shirks when employed enjoys the benefit of a lower expenditure of effort, but pays the cost of spending more time in the unemployment pool. Consider an employed worker with a job paying a wage w. The expected present discounted value of lifetime utility for a shirker can be expressed as:

$$(1)\, V_E^S = w - e_L + (1-b)(1-q)\frac{V_E^S}{1+r} + (b+q-bq)\frac{V_U}{1+r} \Rightarrow V_E^S = \frac{(b+q-bq)V_U + (1+r)(w-e_L)}{b+q-bq+r}$$

To interpret (1), note that in the present period, the shirker receives utility of $w - e_L$. If exogenous separation and being caught shirking are independent events, then the probability that neither one happens (so the shirker is still employed in the next period) is $(1 - b)(1 - q)$. The value of still having a job in the next period is V_E^S, discounted one period to the present. Note that the value of shirking is the same in every period because of the infinite time horizon.[8] If she exogenously separates or is caught shirking, which will occur with probability $(b + q - bq)$, then she will receive a payoff in the next period (also discounted one period to the present) equal to the value of being unemployed.

The expected present discounted value of lifetime utility for a non-shirker is:

$$(2)\qquad V_E^N = w - e_H + (1-b)\frac{V_E^N}{1+r} + b\frac{V_U}{1+r} \Rightarrow V_E^N = \frac{bV_U + (1+r)(w-e_H)}{b+r}$$

The interpretation of this equation is similar to that of (1) above. Current period utility is lower (because effort is higher) but the probability of becoming unemployed is lower as well.

---

[8] The infinite horizon assumption justifies treating V_E as a constant. But one of the goals of this paper is to do comparative statics exercises, which means that the world need not look the same in all periods. The steady-state framework can still be employed, however, by making the assumption that workers maximize *expected* lifetime utility.

The next step is to find an expression for the expected present discounted value of being unemployed V_U. A worker who is currently unemployed will be employed again in future periods,[9] and will receive positive per-period utility in those periods, so this value is strictly positive.

$$(3) \qquad V_U = \bar{u} + a\frac{V_E}{1+r} + (1-a)\frac{V_U}{1+r} \Rightarrow V_U = \frac{aV_E + (1+r)\bar{u}}{a+r}$$

The interpretation of this equation is similar to the ones above. Current period utility is equal to $\bar{u}$, which S&S normalize to zero. In the next period, the worker will find a good job with probability a, or will remain without a good job with probability $(1-a)$.

The value of being unemployed, for shirkers and for non-shirkers respectively, can be expressed as:

$$(4) \qquad V_U^S = \frac{aV_E^S + (1+r)\bar{u}}{a+r}$$

$$(5) \qquad V_U^N = \frac{aV_E^N + (1+r)\bar{u}}{a+r}$$

Combining (1) with (4) and (2) with (5) allows V_E^S and V_E^N to be expressed as functions of exogenous parameters and of the good job acquisition parameter a.

$$(6) \qquad V_E^S = \frac{(1+r)[(b+q-bq)\bar{u} + (a+r)(w-e_L)]}{r(a+b+q-bq+r)}$$

$$(7) \qquad V_E^N = \frac{(1+r)[b\bar{u} + (a+r)(w-e_H)]}{r(a+b+r)}$$

B. The No-Shirk Condition (NSC).

The no-shirk condition (*NSC*) for an individual worker is that $V_E^N > V_E^S$. Define a "good" job as a job with a wage high enough to satisfy the *NSC*. A firm that wishes to offer a good job will

---

[9] Since all workers are identical, there is no stigma associated with having been fired in the past. A worker who was fired for shirking was simply not paid a wage high enough to induce them not to shirk.

pay a wage w_G, which is the lowest wage at which the *NSC* is satisfied. Setting (6) equal to (7) and solving for w, this critical wage can be expressed as:

$$(8) \qquad w_G = \bar{u} + e_H + \frac{(a+b+r)(e_H - e_L)}{q - bq}$$

Equation (8) implies that the critical wage is greater: the smaller the shirking detection probability q; the higher the per-period utility of someone without a good job $\bar{u}$; the higher the good job acquisition rate a; the higher the probability of an exogenous separation b; the higher the discount rate r; the larger the effort of a non-shirker e_H; and the smaller the effort of a shirker e_L.

All of these properties are intuitive. In a good job the penalty for being caught shirking and fired must be sufficiently large that the worker will choose not to shirk. Anything that tends to reduce this penalty causes the critical wage to increase. A lower probability of being caught if shirking, a less painful separation from having a good job, a shorter expected duration without a good job, and higher discounting of the future all tend to lower the penalty. A higher probability of exogenous separation from a good job makes the job less worth protecting, raising the critical wage. A higher effort requirement for a non-shirker and a lower effort requirement for a shirker also make shirking more attractive, which also raises the critical wage.

In a steady-state equilibrium, the flow of workers into good jobs must equal the flow out of good jobs. The flow in must be equal to $a(N - G)$ where N is the number of workers in the economy and G is the number of good jobs. If no one shirks in equilibrium,[10] then the flow out of good jobs is equal to bG where b is the exogenous rate of job separation. In this case, the good job acquisition parameter a can be written as:

---

[10] There cannot be an equilibrium in which workers with good jobs shirk with positive probability. The reason is as follows. There cannot be a pure strategy equilibrium in which all workers with good jobs shirk, because then no good jobs would be offered. There also cannot be a mixed strategy equilibrium in which all workers shirk with probability p; if all workers with good jobs shirked with probability p, then the equilibrium good job wage w_G would reflect that fact. But any firm could get a worker to switch from shirking with probability p to shirking with probability zero by offering a wage infinitesimally higher than w_G.

$$(9) \qquad\qquad\qquad\qquad a = \frac{bG}{N-G}$$

Substituting (9) into (8) gives the no-shirk condition (*NSC*):

$$(10) \qquad\qquad w_G = \bar{u} + e_H + \frac{r(e_H - e_L)}{q - qb} + \frac{bN(e_H - e_L)}{(q - qb)(N - G)}$$

The critical wage is now expressed as a function of exogenous parameters and of G. In order for (10) to hold, it must be the case that workers believe there will be G good jobs, whose holders do not shirk, and that these beliefs are correct in equilibrium. This condition is satisfied because (10) is derived from (9), which is based on the notion that if there are G good jobs offered, firms will offer a wage high enough that no worker with a good job will shirk.

Note that the critical wage is increasing in G. When employment is high, a fired worker can expect to spend less time in the unemployment pool, and therefore requires a higher wage in order to refrain from shirking. Also note that not everyone can have a good job in equilibrium; setting $N = G$ drives the critical wage to infinity. The intuition behind this is that if everyone can get a good job, then workers know that if they are fired from a good job they will be immediately re-hired into another one, so they have no reason to refrain from shirking.

C. Equilibrium.

In the S&S model, shirkers are completely unproductive, which means that no firm would ever have any incentive to offer a job in which workers were not paid enough to satisfy the *NSC*. This means that any worker who does not have a good job is unemployed, and receives the unemployment utility $\bar{u} = 0$. The S&S equilibrium is therefore at the level of employment G and the wage w_G characterized by the intersection of the *NSC* (with $\bar{u} = 0$) and the labor demand curve. The S&S equilibrium is illustrated in Figure 1.

Figure 1: The Shapiro & Stiglitz Equilibrium

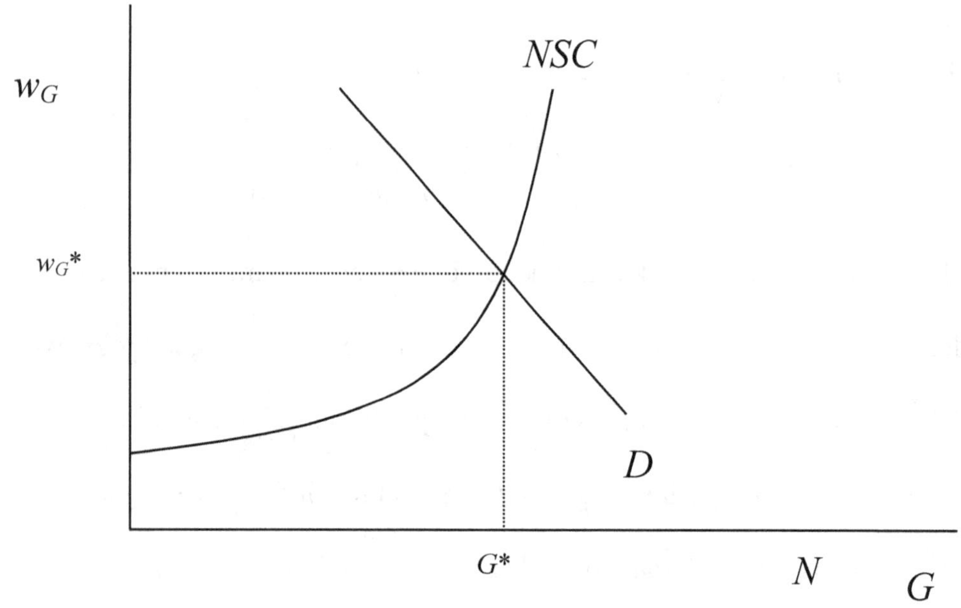

3. Allowing Shirkers to Have Positive Output.

The analysis up to this point has essentially been a restatement of the S&S model. A key assumption in that model is that shirking workers do not produce any output, which means that no firm would ever hire a worker without also paying an efficiency wage high enough to ensure that the worker would not shirk. In contrast, I assume that shirking workers produce a fraction γ as much output as non-shirking workers, which means that $1/\gamma$ shirkers produce as much output as one non-shirker. Define a "bad" job as a job in which a worker is hired, but paid just enough to induce the worker to show up and shirk, and not enough to induce non-shirking. Bad jobs pay a wage of w_B, and do not come with a policy of firing shirkers. As will be shown below, there are some parameter values for which no bad jobs will be offered in equilibrium. However, there are also parameter values for which only bad jobs are offered in equilibrium, as well as parameter values for which both good jobs and bad jobs are offered. I consider each of these cases in turn.

3.1. The Shapiro & Stiglitz Equilibrium (*SSE*).

As discussed above, in the original S&S model shirkers are assumed to produce no output at all. S&S point out, however, that the output of a shirking worker need not be literally zero for the *SSE* to hold, but rather cannot be above some threshold. Specifically, the *SSE* will exist as long as, for the *G* defined by the intersection of the *NSC* and the (unspecified) labor demand function, no firm would prefer to hire a unit of effective labor by offering $1/\gamma$ bad jobs at a total cost of w_B/γ than to offer one good job at a cost of w_G. Since the presence of unemployment in the *SSE* guarantees that $w_B = e_L$ and hence that $\bar{u} = 0$, this condition can be written as:

$$(11) \qquad w_G < \frac{w_B}{\gamma} \Rightarrow w_G < \frac{e_L}{\gamma} \Rightarrow e_H + \frac{r(e_H - e_L)}{q - qb} + \frac{bN(e_H - e_L)}{(q - qb)(N - G)} < \frac{e_L}{\gamma}$$

Equation (11) implicitly defines the threshold of γ below which the *SSE* exists.[11] When the *SSE* holds, equilibrium is as depicted in Figure 1 above. It is easy to see that the condition in (11) gets more difficult to satisfy as *G* increases. As *G* approaches *N*, the left-hand side of the inequality goes to infinity, which means that the condition in (11) can only be satisfied if γ approaches zero. Since *G* is increasing in labor demand this means that the higher is labor demand, the *smaller* is the range of γ over which the *SSE* exists. As labor demand becomes arbitrarily high, the *SSE* can only exist if the output of shirking workers is arbitrarily close to zero. The intuition is that as labor demand increases, w_G in the *SSE* increases as well; when *G* is high, unemployment is low, so workers must be paid a higher wage to induce non-shirking. In contrast, w_B remains the same regardless of the level of labor demand; as long as there is unemployment, w_B remains equal to e_L. Since the cost of filling a good job is increasing in labor demand while the cost of filling a bad job remains constant, offering bad jobs becomes more attractive relative to offering good ones. At some point, a positive number of bad jobs are offered.

---

[11] See the Appendix 1 for proofs of the uniqueness of all equilibria.

i. Effect of Changes in Labor Demand on the SSE.

It is easy to see that higher labor demand causes G, w_G, and total effective labor supplied L (which is proportional to total output in the economy) to increase.[12]

ii. Effect of Changes in γ on the SSE.

Increasing γ has no effect on the left-hand side of the inequality in (11), so as long as (11) holds, increasing γ has no effect on employment, wages, or output. When γ gets big enough, (11) will no longer hold and a positive number of bad jobs will be offered in equilibrium.

3.2. The "Everyone Shirks" Equilibrium (*ESE*).

In the *SSE* only good jobs exist. The opposite extreme is an equilibrium in which only bad jobs exist. I refer to this as an "Everyone Shirks" equilibrium or *ESE*. As will become clear below, *ESE* equilibria may or may not involve unemployment.

A. The "Everyone Shirks" Equilibrium with Unemployment (ESE^{UE}).

Two conditions must hold for the *ESE^{UE}* to exist. First, labor demand must be too low to generate full employment, conditional on all jobs in the economy being bad jobs. That is:

$$(12a) \qquad\qquad D(\gamma N) < \frac{e_L}{\gamma}$$

The function $D(\cdot)$ represents demand for effective labor. Equation (12a) can be seen graphically in Figure 2 below. If all jobs in the economy are bad jobs, then the maximum possible labor supply is γN units of effective labor. The wage if there is unemployment will be e_L, and so the cost

---

[12] In the *SSE*, L is simply equal to G. As will be seen below, when there are B bad jobs in equilibrium, L will be equal to $G + \gamma B$.

of hiring a unit of effective labor by offering $1/\gamma$ bad jobs will be e_L/γ, which is represented in Figure 2 by the horizontal line segment. If labor demand is low enough that it intersects with the horizontal line segment to the left of γN, then there will be unemployment in the economy.

The second condition is that firms must in fact prefer offering $1/\gamma$ bad jobs to offering one good job even when $G = 0$ and $\bar{u} = 0$ (which is when w_G is smallest). That is:

$$(12b) \qquad w_G > \frac{w_B}{\gamma} \Rightarrow w_G > \frac{e_L}{\gamma} \Rightarrow e_H + \frac{(b+r)(e_H - e_L)}{q - qb} > \frac{e_L}{\gamma}$$

i. Effect of Changes in Labor Demand on the ESE^{UE}.

As long as (12) holds, an increase in labor demand has no effect on w_B (it remains fixed at e_L), so wages are a-cyclical in the ESE^{UE}. The only effect of an increase in labor demand is an increase in B and in total effective labor supplied $L = \gamma B$.

ii. Effect of Changes in γ on the ESE^{UE}.

When there is unemployment in the economy, w_B is fixed at e_L. So increasing γ decreases the cost of a unit of effective labor (i.e., the horizontal line in Figure 2 shifts down), which causes an increase in the quantity of effective labor supplied L. The effect of an increase in γ on B is ambiguous (proof in Appendix 2).[13] The intuition is that total effective labor hired increases, but each worker has also gotten more productive. If labor demand is very steep, then the increase in total effective labor demanded will be small, and B will decrease. The reverse holds if labor demand is very flat.

---

[13] All comparative statics proofs in this paper are of the same form; totally differentiate the system of equations that defines the equilibrium, set the resulting expressions equal to zero, and solve the resulting system for the comparative statics derivatives. Appendix 2 contains proofs for a few of these exercises. The remainder are available from the author upon request.

Figure 2: The "Everyone Shirks" Equilibrium

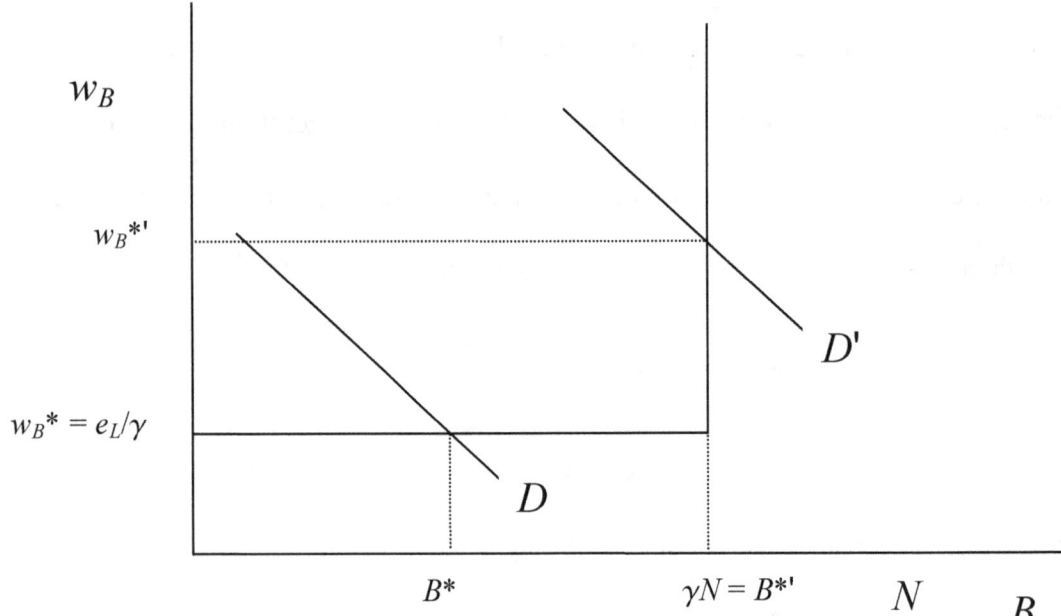

For γ sufficiently large, the inequality in (12b) must hold, so the ESE^{UE} will hold as long as labor demand is sufficiently low. If (12b) is satisfied at a given level of labor demand, then increasing γ can never cause it not to hold.

B. The "Everyone Shirks" Equilibrium with Full Employment (ESE^{FE}).

Two conditions must hold for the ESE^{FE} to exist. First, labor demand must be high enough to generate full employment, conditional on all jobs in the economy being bad jobs.

$$(13a) \qquad\qquad D(\gamma N) > \frac{e_L}{\gamma}$$

This requirement can be seen graphically in Figure 2. If all jobs in the economy are bad jobs, then there will be full employment as long as labor demand intersects the vertical line at γN at a height above e_L/γ. Full employment drives w_B above e_L.

The second condition is that firms must in fact prefer offering $1/\gamma$ bad jobs to offering one good job when $G = 0$ and $\bar{u} = w_B - e_L > 0$. That is:

$$(13b) \qquad w_G > \frac{w_B}{\gamma} \Rightarrow e_H + w_B - e_L + \frac{(b+r)(e_H - e_L)}{q - qb} > \frac{w_B}{\gamma}$$

The w_B in (13b) is not an exogenous parameter, but rather is implicitly defined by the labor demand function. An increase in labor demand sufficient to cause a one-unit increase in w_B will cause the left-hand side of the inequality in (13b) to increase by one unit, and will cause the right-hand side to increase by $1/\gamma > 1$ units. When w_B gets big enough, (13b) no longer holds. So the higher is labor demand, the smaller is the range of γ over which the ESE^{FE} holds. As labor demand becomes arbitrarily high, the ESE^{FE} can only exist if the output of shirking workers is arbitrarily close to the output of non-shirking workers. The intuition is that for every one-dollar increase in w_B as a result of increased labor demand, $\bar{u}$ in the NSC increases by one dollar as well, so a one-dollar increase in w_B makes both good jobs and bad jobs more expensive to fill by one dollar. Since workers in good jobs are more productive, increases in w_B make offering good jobs relatively more attractive.

i. Effect of Changes in Labor Demand on the ESE^{FE}.

It is clear from Figure 2 that, as long as it does not cause the ESE^{FE} to cease to hold, an increase in labor demand will have no effect on B (there is already full employment) or L, and will cause w_B to increase.

ii. Effect of Changes in γ on the ESE^{FE}.

An increase in γ causes the supply of effective labor to increase. As long as full employment is maintained, this can have no effect on B, but must cause L to increase. The effect on w_B is ambiguous (proof in Appendix 2). An increase in γ causes each bad-job worker to generate more

17

effective labor, which tends to increase w_B. On the other hand, the increase in L reduces the price per unit of effective labor. The net effect is ambiguous.

Higher γ makes offering bad jobs more attractive relative to offering good jobs, so increasing γ will never cause a switch to an equilibrium with a positive number of good jobs. It can, however, cause a switch to the ESE^{UE} if labor demand is too low to support full employment at the new, higher supply of effective labor.

3.3. The Intermediate Equilibrium (*IE*).

We saw above that for the *SSE* to hold, γ must be low enough that firms offer no bad jobs even when $G > 0$ and w_G is correspondingly high. We also saw that the *ESE* to hold, γ must be high enough that firms offer no good jobs even when $G = 0$ and w_G is correspondingly low. At intermediate levels of γ neither of these conditions can be satisfied, which means that there must be a positive number of both good jobs and bad jobs. For this to be true in equilibrium, it must be the case that firms are indifferent between offering one good job or offering $1/\gamma$ bad jobs.

I refer to this as the "Intermediate Equilibrium" (*IE*). To see the intuition behind the *IE*, start at the intersection between the *NSC* and the labor demand curve in Figure 1. If (11) is not satisfied, then the *SSE* cannot be an equilibrium; an employer would want to deviate by eliminating a good job and replacing it with $1/\gamma$ bad jobs. The workers in these bad jobs would be hired out of the unemployment pool so $w_B = e_L$. Now imagine that one firm deviates and offers $1/\gamma$ bad jobs instead. These workers supply one unit of effective labor, so the relevant demand for workers to fill good jobs is the residual demand $1/\gamma$ units lower than the original demand.[14] This lower demand causes a decrease in w_G, which makes offering good jobs more attractive. This process of

_____

[14] The *NSC* would be unaffected because $\bar{u}$ would still be equal to zero.

18

replacing good jobs with bad jobs would continue until the indifference between the two types of jobs was restored.

As discussed above, when labor demand increases, the conditions for the *SSE* and the conditions for the *ESE* become more difficult to satisfy. This means that when labor demand is high, the range of γ over which the *IE* exists gets larger. As labor demand becomes arbitrarily high, the *IE* exists for almost all values of $\gamma \in (0,1)$. As in the *ESE*, there may or may not be unemployment in the *IE*, depending on the level of labor demand.

A. The Intermediate Equilibrium with Unemployment (IE^{UE}).

When the IE^{UE} equilibrium (in which there is unemployment) exists, the following conditions must hold:

$$(14a) \qquad\qquad w_G = \frac{e_L}{\gamma}$$

$$(14b) \qquad\qquad w_G = e_H + \frac{r(e_H - e_L)}{q - qb} + \frac{bN(e_H - e_L)}{(q - qb)(N - G)}$$

Equation (14a) must hold because in the *IE* firms must be indifferent between offering one good job and offering $1/\gamma$ bad jobs; and because if there is unemployment, a bad job can be filled at a wage of e_L. Equation (14b) must hold because the *NSC* (with $\bar{u} = 0$, because there is unemployment) must be satisfied if there are to be $G > 0$ good jobs in equilibrium.

i. Effect of Changes in Labor Demand on the IE^{UE}.

As long as it does not get high enough that the IE^{UE} ceases to hold, an increase in labor demand has no effect on w_B, and from (14a) it is clear that it also has no effect on w_G. From (14b) it is clear that fixing w_G also means fixing G, so the only effect in the IE^{UE} of an increase in labor demand is that B increases, which causes $L = G + \gamma B$ to increase as well. The increase in the number of bad jobs causes the average wage $w_{AVG} = \dfrac{w_G G + w_B B}{G + B}$ to fall. So in the IE^{UE}, wages are counter-cyclical.

ii. Effect of Changes in γ on the IE^{UE}.

Since there is unemployment in the economy, w_B is fixed at e_L. An increase in γ breaks the indifference between offering one good job and offering $1/\gamma$ bad jobs, causing some firms to switch from good jobs to bad. This causes G to decrease. The effect on B is ambiguous (proof in Appendix 2). The intuition is as follows. The reduction in G increases the residual demand for bad-job workers, which tends to increase B. At the same time, each shirking worker has become more productive, which tends to decrease B. The effect of an increase in γ on L is unambiguously positive (proof in Appendix 2). The intuition is that in the IE^{UE}, each unit of effective labor costs e_L/γ, regardless of whether it comes from one non-shirker or from $1/\gamma$. When γ is larger, effective labor becomes cheaper, and so more effective labor is supplied.

B. The Intermediate Equilibrium with Full Employment (IE^{FE}).

If labor demand is sufficiently high, then there will be full employment in equilibrium; there will be G good jobs and $N - G$ bad jobs, which supply a total of $\gamma(N - G)$ units of effective labor. The equilibrium levels of G, w_G, B, and w_B are determined by the following:

(15a)
$$w_G = \frac{w_B}{\gamma} = D(G + \gamma B)$$

(15b)
$$w_G = e_H + w_B - e_L + \frac{r(e_H - e_L)}{q - qb} + \frac{bN(e_H - e_L)}{(q - qb)(N - G)}$$

This system is similar to (14) above, except that now $w_B > e_L$ and so $\bar{u}$ is equal to $w_B - e_L > 0$, instead of being fixed at zero. $D(\bullet)$ represents the total demand for effective labor, and (15a) represents the requirement that in equilibrium w_G is determined by the intersection of *NSC* and the residual demand curve (after γB has been subtracted out).

i. Effect of Changes in Labor Demand on the IE^{FE}.

In the IE^{FE}, firms cannot hire more workers out of the unemployment pool in response to an increase in labor demand; the only way to increase the amount of effective labor is to convert shirking workers into non-shirking workers by offering a higher good-job wage. This causes G to increase, which must mean that B decreases, because $G + B = N$ when there is no unemployment. The higher labor demand, combined with the switch from bad jobs to good jobs, must cause both w_B and w_G (and hence w_{AVG}) to increase. The intuition is that the higher labor demand cannot increase employment; it can only cause a reallocation of workers from bad jobs to good jobs, while putting upward pressure on wages for both kinds of jobs.

ii. Effect of Changes in γ on the IE^{FE}.

An increase in γ causes the marginal firm to want to substitute bad jobs for good jobs, increasing B and reducing G. The net effect on L is ambiguous; some non-shirkers have been replaced by shirkers, but all shirkers have become more productive. The effect on w_G and on w_B is ambiguous as well (proof in Appendix 2). To see this, consider the case where the net effect on L is zero. Since the total amount of effective labor supplied is constant, the price of a unit of effective labor must be constant as well. That is, w_G and w_B/γ must be constants. Since γ is larger, w_B must also be larger. If the net effect on L is positive, then the price of a unit of effective labor must fall, which means that w_G must fall and the effect on w_B is ambiguous. If the net effect on L is negative, then the price of a unit of effective labor must rise, which means that both w_G and w_B must rise.

4. Empirical Implications:

A. Cyclicality of Wages.

There is an empirical literature on the question of whether or not wages are pro-cyclical, the results of which are mixed.[15] This paper may make some contribution to resolving that ambiguity in the data, as model makes testable predictions about when wages are pro-cyclical, counter-cyclical, or a-cyclical. In the SSE, ESE^{FE}, and IE^{FE}, wages are pro-cyclical; higher labor demand causes higher average wages. In the ESE^{UE} wages are a-cyclical; higher labor demand has no effect on average wages. In the IE^{UE}, increases in labor demand have no effect on bad-job wages or on good-job wages, but they increase the number of bad jobs in the economy and have no effect on the number of good jobs, so average wages fall. It remains an open empirical question whether the specific predictions of the model can resolve any part of the ambiguity in the empirical literature.

B. Technological Change.

The key parameter in the model is γ, which represents the ratio of the output of a non-shirker to that of a shirker. If γ is in fact an important determinant of economic outcomes, then any economic change that influences γ may be important as well. The model makes explicit predictions regarding the effect on employment, wages, and output of productivity improvements that take the form of an increase in the output of shirkers (holding the output of non-shirkers constant),

---

[15] See Abraham and Haltiwanger (1995) for a survey.

and shows how the effects depend on which equilibrium the economy is in. More generally, the model suggests that the effects of technological progress will depend in part on whether it is γ-increasing, γ-decreasing, or γ-neutral. Embedding this idea in a more general model of technological progress is a possible subject for future research.

5. Conclusion:

The Shapiro & Stiglitz paper is a seminal contribution to the efficiency wage literature. It develops a model featuring equilibrium unemployment that arises as a consequence of imperfect monitoring of worker effort. In their model, S&S assume that shirking workers produce no output. In this paper, I allow the productivity of shirking workers to range from zero to a level equal to that of non-shirkers. The model predicts that if shirking workers are sufficiently productive relative to non-shirkers, then some (or all) workers in the economy will be hired into jobs that do not pay an efficiency wage and in which shirking is tolerated. Comparative statics on this richer model show that the effects of changes in labor demand and in the productivity of shirkers relative to non-shirkers on economic performance depend on which equilibrium the economy is in.

Appendix 1: Uniqueness Proofs

Proof that the SSE is Unique:
When (11) is satisfied, there cannot be an alternative equilibrium to the *SSE* in which there is unemployment. The reason is that as long as there is unemployment in the economy, it must be the case that $w_B = e_L$, which means that $\bar{u} = 0$ and the *NSC* is the same as in the *SSE*. Any substitution of bad jobs for good jobs would cause the residual demand for good jobs to fall, which would make w_G fall as well. Since no firm wants to offer any bad jobs at the original w_G, no firm will want to offer them at a lower w_G.

When (11) is satisfied, there also cannot be an alternative equilibrium to the *SSE* in which there is full employment. If there were full employment, it would have to be the case that $\bar{u} > 0$. In any candidate equilibrium with $G > 0$ and $\bar{u} > 0$, the cost of hiring a unit of effective labor by offering $1/\gamma$ bad jobs is greater than in the *SSE* by $\bar{u}/\gamma$. In contrast, it is clear from (10) that the cost of hiring a unit of effective labor by offering a good job, holding G constant, only increases by $\bar{u} < \bar{u}/\gamma$. So offering a bad job is relatively less attractive than in the *SSE*, and no firm does it in the *SSE*. The existence of bad jobs will also reduce residual demand for good jobs, which will reduce w_G, making offering bad jobs less attractive still.

$\square$

Proof that the ESE is Unique:
If the conditions for the *ESE* to exist are satisfied, then all firms prefer offering $1/\gamma$ bad jobs to offering one good job when $G = 0$. There can only be one equilibrium where $G = 0$, because the labor demand curve can only cross the $G = 0$ labor supply function once (see Figure 2). So the only possible alternative equilibrium is one in which $G > 0$. Consider a proposed alternative equilibrium in which $G = G^{ALT} > 0$ and $w_B = w_B^{ALT}$. We know that for the *ESE* to exist, it must be the case that:

$$(A1) \qquad w_G^{ES} > \frac{w_B^{ES}}{\gamma} \Rightarrow w_G^{ES} - \frac{w_B^{ES}}{\gamma} > 0$$

In order for the alternative equilibrium to exist, it must be the case that:

$$(A2) \qquad w_G^{ALT} < \frac{w_B^{ALT}}{\gamma} \Rightarrow w_G^{ALT} - \frac{w_B^{ALT}}{\gamma} < 0$$

A necessary condition for (A2) to be true given that (A1) is true is:

$$(A3) \qquad \left(w_G^{ES} - \frac{w_B^{ES}}{\gamma} \right) - \left(w_G^{ALT} - \frac{w_B^{ALT}}{\gamma} \right) > 0$$

In any equilibrium where $G > 0$, the NSC must be satisfied. Substituting (14b) for w_G^{ES} and for w_G^{ALT}, and using the fact that $G^{ES} = 0$, ($A3$) becomes:

($A4$)
$$\frac{(w_B^{ALT} - w_B^{ES})}{\gamma} - \frac{b(e_H - e_L)G^{ALT}}{q(1-b)(N - G^{ALT})} > 0$$

The second term in ($A4$) is positive. So for ($A4$) to hold, the first term must be positive, which requires that $w_B^{ALT} > w_B^{ES}$. But this cannot be true; $G^{ALT} > 0$ reduces the residual demand for bad-job workers, which cannot increase the bad-job wage.

□

Proof that the IE is Unique:
Using (15b) and rearranging slightly, we see that for the IE to hold, it must be the case that:

($A5$)
$$w_G^{IE} = \frac{w_B^{IE}}{\gamma} \Rightarrow e_H - e_L + \frac{r(e_H - e_L)}{q - qb} + \frac{bN(e_H - e_L)}{(q - qb)(N - G^{IE})} = \frac{(1-\gamma)w_B^{IE}}{\gamma}$$

For an alternative equilibrium to characterized by $G > 0$ and $B > 0$ to exist, it would have to be the case that:

($A6$)
$$w_G^{ALT} = \frac{w_B^{ALT}}{\gamma} \Rightarrow e_H - e_L + \frac{r(e_H - e_L)}{q - qb} + \frac{bN(e_H - e_L)}{(q - qb)(N - G^{ALT})} = \frac{(1-\gamma)w_B^{ALT}}{\gamma}$$

Consider a proposed alternative equilibrium in which $G = G^{ALT} > 0$ and $w_B = w_B^{ALT}$. If $G^{ALT} > G^{IE}$, then the left-hand side of ($A6$) will be larger than the corresponding term in ($A5$). In order for ($A6$) to hold, given that ($A5$) holds, the right-hand side would have to be larger as well, which would require that $w_B^{ALT} > w_B^{IE}$. But the increase in G reduces the residual demand for bad jobs, so this cannot be true. The same analysis holds for $G^{ALT} < G^{IE}$.

The only other possible alternative equilibria are those for which $G = 0$ or $B = 0$. But we know that if $B = 0$, firms prefer offering $1/\gamma$ bad jobs to offering one good job. Similarly, we know that if $G = 0$, firms prefer offering one good job to offering $1/\gamma$ bad jobs.

□

Appendix 2: Comparative Statics Proofs

Proof that the Effect of an Increase in γ on B is Ambiguous in the ESE^{UE}:
The number of bad jobs B is equal to L/γ. The total derivative of L/γ with respect to γ is:

($A7$)
$$\frac{\gamma \dfrac{dL}{d\gamma} - L}{\gamma^2}$$

As discussed in the text, $dL/d\gamma > 0$, so the sign of ($A7$) is ambiguous. It is straightforward to find examples where ($A7$) can be of either sign when the parameter restrictions necessary for the ESE^{UE} to exist are satisfied.

□

Proof that the Effect of an Increase in γ on w_B is Ambiguous in the ESE^{FE}:
The bad-job wage w_B is equal to $\gamma D(\gamma N)$. The total derivative of $\gamma D(\gamma N)$ with respect to γ is:

$$(A8) \qquad\qquad D(\gamma N) + \gamma N D'(\gamma N)$$

Since D is downward-sloping, the sign of ($A8$) is ambiguous. It is straightforward to find examples where ($A8$) can be of either sign when the parameter restrictions necessary for the ESE^{FE} to exist are satisfied.

□

Proof that the Effect of an Increase in γ on B is Ambiguous in the $\mathbf{IE}^{UE}$:
Totally differentiating ($14a$) and ($14b$) with respect to γ and solving gives:

$$(A9) \qquad \frac{dB}{d\gamma} = \frac{qe_L(1-b)(G-N)^2}{b\gamma^3 N(e_H - e_L)} - \frac{B}{\gamma} - \frac{e_L}{\gamma^3 D'(G + \gamma B)}$$

The first and second terms in ($A9$) are positive, and the third term is negative. The sign of the expression is ambiguous. It is straightforward to find examples where ($A9$) can be of either sign when the parameter restrictions necessary for the IE^{FE} to exist are satisfied.

□

Proof that an Increase in γ Causes L to Increase $\mathbf{IE}^{UE}$:
Totally differentiating ($14a$) and ($14b$) with respect to γ and solving gives:

$$(A10) \qquad \frac{dL}{d\gamma} = \frac{d(G + \gamma B)}{d\gamma} = B + \gamma\frac{dB}{d\gamma} + \frac{dG}{d\gamma} = -\frac{e_L}{\gamma^2 D'(G + \gamma B)}$$

The expression in ($A10$) is unambiguously positive.

□

References:

Abraham, Katharine G., and Haltiwanger, John C. "Real Wages and the Business Cycle" *Journal of Economic Literature* 33 (1995): 1215-64.

Bulow, Jeremy I., and Summers, Lawrence H. "A Theory of Dual Labor Markets with Application to Industrial Policy, Discrimination, and Keynesian Unemployment" *Journal of Labor Economics* 4 (1986): 376-414.

Levine, David I. "Just-Cause Employment Policies When Unemployment Is a Worker Discipline Device" *American Economic Review* 79 (1989): 902-05.

MacLeod, Bentley, and Malcomson, James M. "Motivation and Markets" *American Economic Review* 88 (1998): 388-411.

Shapiro, Carl, and Stiglitz, Joseph E. "Equilibrium Unemployment as a Worker Discipline Device" *American Economic Review* 74 (1984): 433-44.

Strand, Jon. "Unemployment as a Discipline Device with Heterogeneous Labor" *American Economic Review* 77 (1987): 489-93.